GREAT MEN OF SCIENCE

WARWICK PRESS

Contents

Left panel, top: Analysis on a special scanning table of the tracks of atomic particles taken by a heavy liquid bubble chamber. Center: One of the Apollo 12 crew sets up an experimental package on the Moon's surface. Bottom: A celestial sphere.

Cover: Michael Faraday demonstrates the principles of electricity at the Royal Institution.

Title page: An analytical balance of 1870. The balance is an important laboratory tool for chemists.

Authors
Edward Holmes
Christopher Maynard

Editor
Jennifer L. Justice

Illustrations
Oliver Frey

Published 1979 by Warwick Press Inc.
730 Fifth Avenue, New York, New York 10019

First published in Great Britain by Purnell Books, in 1975

Copyright © 1975 by Grisewood & Dempsey Ltd.

Printed in Italy by New Interlitho, Milan

Library of Congress Catalog Card No. 78-68533
ISBN 0-531-09150-3

Great Men of Science

Science is the knowledge of general truths and universal laws gained by observation, testing, and recording. And the story of science is the story of men with enquiring minds who have sought to explain the world about them.

The great men of science are those who combined the work of their predecessors and their own observations with such genius that they arrived at theories which revolutionized Man's understanding of his world. Men like Copernicus, Newton, and Darwin overturned prevailing ideas about Man and the universe. Other men, like Carolus Linnaeus, spent their lives classifying existing knowledge and sweeping away many of the misconceptions of the past.

Many of the great scientists were men of imagination and foresight who applied their findings to solving practical problems. For the line between pure science – researching and recording for its own sake – and technology, the application of that research, is often a thin one.

Great Men of Science traces the story of some of these men and their work, from the investigations into astronomy and medicine of the ancient world to the research into subatomic particles and the mysteries of the double helix of DNA.

Above: An early microscope – a tool which opened up whole new areas of research. Below: "Experiment with a Bird in the Air Pump", by Joseph Wright (1734–1797). Such experiments were among the earliest investigations into the gases that make up the air.

The Story of Science

The history of science begins with Man's first attempts to find a constant pattern in the world around him.

The earliest men had no time for science. Their wandering and hunting way of life was a grim struggle for survival, and they had few opportunities to ponder on the reasons for what happened around them. But then Man changed from a hunter to a farmer, and the story of science begins.

These were agricultural communities, so the timing of the seasons was immensely important. Men learnt to tell the time of year by the position of the stars – and from their observations grew the science of astronomy. Another very early and practical science was geometry, used in building and marking out land.

As civilizations developed and life became easier, the early scientists had time to think about the working of the universe. At first they were inclined to explain what they could not account for as the whim of a god. But the early Greek thinkers tried to find other explanations.

In prehistoric times men made life-like paintings of animals on the walls of caves. These may have played a part in magic rituals.

Their attitude was scientific: they believed in observing and noting facts, and undertaking experiments. They built on the knowledge of earlier peoples, but believed that such knowledge should be checked by what they could see for themselves.

The Greek schools of science still flourished under the Roman Empire. But when the Empire crumbled, men had little time for science. Most of their books were destroyed. Although in the East the development of science continued unchecked, in Europe it was eclipsed with the coming of the Dark Ages. But the Arabs preserved the Greek learning and built on it; and through translations of Arab works science returned to Europe from about the 10th century.

The people of the Middle Ages believed in authority. Their views on religion they took from the Church

Top: In the Dark Ages organized science in Europe came to a halt. But in the Near East the alchemists laid the foundations of modern chemistry. Alchemy spread to Europe and did not die out until well after the Renaissance.
Above: The invention of the wheel in prehistoric times gave Man an invaluable tool for technology and science.

Isaac Newton (1642–1727) was the first to set out the laws of the universe. His most important work was done before he was 30 years old.

leaders; similarly they accepted the Greek scientific theories in an unquestioning way. But with the Renaissance came a new spirit of enquiry. The power of the Church was defied by Martin Luther; and Nicolaus Copernicus flatly contradicted Ptolemy by saying that the Sun and not the Earth was the center of the universe.

During the Renaissance learning became fashionable. The invention of printing brought the new ideas within the reach of scholars all over Europe. At this time, too, new tools were invented which were an immense help to

Above: In the 18th century science was a fashionable study, and society was intrigued by such experiments as this early demonstration of electricity.

Below: The development of the microscope in the late 1600s opened men's eyes to undreamed forms of life.

scientists. With his telescope Galileo discovered new heavenly bodies; with his microscopes Leeuwenhoek studied the teeming bacteria in a drop of water.

Leeuwenhoek's works were published by the Royal Society in London. Here, men met to discuss subjects ranging from "valves in the veins" to "the weight of air". Its members included Robert Boyle, the eminent chemist, the astronomer Halley, and later Humphry Davy and Lord Rutherford, among many others. But most famous of all was Isaac Newton, whose laws of gravity and motion were the first really systematic setting out of the laws governing the universe.

The 18th century was the Age of Reason – and this was the ideal outlook for scientists. Enormous strides were made in chemistry and experiments with electricity began. The fashion for reason and order led to the classification of

physical laws, chemical elements, and living things.

This was the age of the amateur scientist; and, as so little was known, it was still possible for one man to have a grasp of all the current knowledge in one quite broad field. But in the 19th century so many advances were made that science became the study of dedicated professionals in ever-narrowing fields. Today new tools – the radio telescope and the electron microscope – enable men to study farther horizons and minuter details than the scientists of even a hundred years ago would have dreamed possible.

But whatever the subject of study, the method of the scientist is unchanging: the observation and classification of facts, and finding their place in the order of nature.

A model of the double helix of DNA – the material from which genes are made. The discovery of this complicated nucleic material may eventually lead to an understanding of how life began.

The Ancient World

Above: The cuneiform or wedge-shaped writing invented by the Sumerians. Writing enabled knowledge to be permanently recorded.

Below: The Great Pyramid – a monument to the skill of Egypt's architects. To construct the building, over two million $2\frac{1}{2}$-ton stone blocks were somehow hauled across the sands and then positioned with unbelievable accuracy.

In the great agricultural civilizations Mesopotamia and Egypt, science grew out of the practical problems of farming and building and was closely linked with religion.

Along the banks of the river Nile and in the land watered by the Tigris and Euphrates grew up two of the greatest early civilizations – those of Egypt and Sumeria, which flourished from about 3000 BC.

Science in Sumeria

We know from excavations that the Sumerians built such great cities as Ur and Babylon. To do so called for some knowledge of scientific techniques. They probably used the wheel to transport the heavy building materials needed to construct the massive city walls. In order to lay out their cities and temples so accurately they must have understood the principles of simple geometry.

The Sumerians had other scientific skills than those needed for planning and building. They believed that the stars controlled the destiny of mankind, and this led them to learn about the movements of stars and planets. Sumerian astrologers – men who predict the course of human affairs from the position of heavenly bodies – were therefore men of great power. The astrologers were part priests, part scientists; science and superstition combined made up Sumerian religion.

The Sumerians were among the first to learn to calculate, and invented a symbol for the number 10 so that large numbers could be written more easily. It is to the Sumerians that we owe the division of the circle into 360 parts, or degrees, still used today.

Slaves carrying earth to make mud bricks for an Assyrian king's palace. Early civilizations depended on huge work forces.

The Sumerians' greatest contribution to science was writing. They invented a complicated script which was pressed on to clay in cuneiform (wedge-shaped) symbols.

On the banks of the Nile

Life in Egypt was centered around the annual flooding of the Nile. Each year boundaries were washed away and had to be relocated by taking measurements from permanent landmarks. To make

The great civilization of Egypt developed from farming communities. The rich soil was worked by ox-drawn plows.

These simple tools, including a mallet and chisels, were used by the craftsmen and farmers of ancient Egypt.

these calculations and work out land areas the Egyptians invented geometry. Their geometry was so accurate that they built the Great Pyramid at Giza with a maximum error of only about a twentieth of a degree. In astronomy the Egyptians made such accurate observations that they realized the year is $365\frac{1}{4}$ days long – although they continued to use a 365-day calendar. They believed that the Sun was the controlling influence on men's lives and, as in Sumeria, the magic of the priests and the science of the astronomers merged to become Egyptian religion.

The Egyptians were also advanced in the science of medicine. They mummified their dead, and in the process learned much about human anatomy. Their practical ability, however, was founded on superstition, and the belief that the god Horus looked after good health.

The Egyptians also recorded their knowledge, using pictorial characters, or hieroglyphs. It was this ability that set the Sumerians and Egyptians apart from others. Scientific knowledge could now be passed on to future generations.

An Egyptian fresco from a tomb at Thebes. It shows (top) the boundaries of a farmer's land being measured – an event that took place every year after the Nile's flooding.
Below: The prehistoric monument of Stonehenge, England, may have been an astronomical observatory.

THE ROYAL CUBIT
Egyptian measurements were based on the *royal cubit*, the distance from the tip of the middle finger to the elbow (about 21 inches, 53 cm). This was divided into 7 *palms* (each about 3 inches, 7·5 cm) and 28 *fingers* (about $\frac{3}{4}$ inch, 2 cm).

Egyptian multiplication was very tedious. The mathematicians were only able to double numbers and multiply by 10. To multiply 3 by 18, for example, they would have to multiply 3 by 2 four times, and 3 by 10 once. The sum of all the products would provide the answer.

Natural Science and the Greeks

Above: The Greek philosopher Aristotle (384–322 BC) laid the foundations of many of the sciences of today.

Below: Part of the Acropolis in Athens. During Greece's Golden Age, many masterpieces of architecture were built. The Greeks were skilled builders who used their knowledge of geometry to create buildings of elegance.

The philosophers of Ancient Greece speculated about the composition of matter and the structure of the universe, and tried to discover the laws of nature.

Most primitive peoples try to explain the workings of the universe in terms of the actions of gods. But the Greek thinkers wanted to explain things mechanically – leaving the gods out of it. Anaxagoras of Clazomenae boldly claimed that the Sun and Moon were nothing but lumps of rock, while Xenophanes of Colophon studied fossils and suggested that the Earth had once been covered with mud. Democritus believed that matter was made up of tiny, indivisible components: he coined the term "atom", meaning "that which cannot be split".

A center of learning and culture

In the 5th century BC, the most illustrious period in Greek history, the center of culture and learning was Athens. The Athenians loved to spend their spare time discussing science and philosophy, and many traveling teachers – called sophists – visited the city, giving lectures on such topics as mathematics, geometry, and astronomy.

In the 4th century BC the philosopher Plato made Athens the first university city in the world when he founded his Academy. His pupil, Aristotle, wrote a series of treatises on natural science, including two books on plants and another on the movement of animals. He put together what was then known of science and added some of his own ideas on biology.

In general the early Greeks were better at abstract thinking than at carrying out practical experiments and inventing labor-saving devices. This was

partly because all Greek societies contained a slave class; the slaves did most of the hard work, leaving educated men free to ponder at leisure. But after mainland Greece had fallen to Alexander the Great, and Alexandria in Egypt became the center of Hellenistic (Greek-based) learning, there was a great explosion of practical knowledge. Euclid set out his theories of geometry which formed the basis of its study until the 20th century. Archimedes not only studied geometrical figures but made many ingenious machines, including a screw for raising water which is still used today. Medical knowledge reached a peak in the 2nd century AD, with the work of Galen.

Below: The frontispiece of the 1496 edition of Ptolemy's "The Almagest", showing the author (left) and the German astronomer Johann Müller. Above them is a sphere with the Earth in the center and the signs of the Zodiac around it.

GREEK SCIENTISTS AND PHILOSOPHERS

700 BC

600 BC

THALES
ANAXIMANDER (born c. 640–
ANAXIMENES 600 BC)

The founding fathers of Greek science. These men continued the mathematical and astronomical traditions of Egypt and Mesopotamia, and in their own right speculated about the nature and creation of matter.

PYTHAGORAS
(c. 580–500 BC)

Laid the foundations of modern geometry.

500 BC

ANAXAGORAS
(born c. 500 BC)

Held that the Sun and stars were not gods, but material objects.

DEMOCRITUS
(born 460 BC)

Suggested that everything was made up of atoms – minute particles of matter.

HIPPOCRATES
(born 460 BC)

The father of medicine; first applied scientific observation to disease.

400 BC

PLATO
(429–348 BC)

The greatest of the Greek philosophers. Plato is important in the history of science because of his belief that all studies should be approached in the same rational way as mathematics.

ARISTOTLE
(384–322 BC)

Plato's pupil. He tried to systematize the whole of human knowledge. His researches into animals formed the basis of medicine and natural history until the Renaissance, nearly 2000 years later.

EUCLID
(born 330 BC)

300 BC

ARISTARCHUS
(born 310 BC)

Systematized the science of geometry; mathematicians still call the most basic sort of geometry after him.

ARCHIMEDES
(c. 287–212 BC)

Established the idea of a Sun-centered universe, a theory which Copernicus revived centuries later.

ERATOSTHENES
(born 275 BC)

Could be called the greatest solver of problems. Best known for his discovery of the principles of leverage, the displacement of water, and the calculation of the area of a circle.

200 BC

HIPPARCHUS
(born 190 BC)

Did much to put geography and the measurement of time on a scientific basis, and devised a system for measuring the Earth.

Worked out the mathematics of planetary movement; his calculations were not improved on until the time of Copernicus.

100 BC

0

HERO (? 'AD)

A shadowy figure; it is not known when he lived, but his writings show him to have been a notable "mechanic", creating ingenious devices like slot machines and the first steam turbine.

AD 100

PTOLEMY
(c. 100–160 AD)

Calculated the size and distance from Earth of the Sun and the Moon.

AD 200

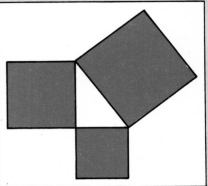

Pythagoras' theorem states that the square on the longest side of a right-angled triangle equals the sum of the squares on the other two sides.

Archimedes showed that a floating ship weighs the same as the water it displaces.

Ptolomy stated that the heavenly bodies orbit the Earth – in the order Moon, Mercury, Venus, Sun, Mars, Jupiter, Saturn.

9

Light in the Dark Ages

Science and learning were almost lost to the West
when the Roman Empire fell to the barbarian hordes.
But the progress of knowledge continued in the East –
in India, China, and, later, the Arab world.

In the 4th century BC the city of Alexandria in Egypt became the center of Greek learning, and over the next 300 years its Museum grew into a treasure house of ancient knowledge. At its peak the Museum's great library contained some 70,000 volumes. When the city was besieged by the Romans in 47 BC the library was destroyed, but a "daughter library" grew up, based on manuscripts given by the Roman Mark Antony. This was also destroyed, on the orders of Emperor Theodosius I, in AD 390, and with it was lost centuries of hard-won knowledge.

At the time the Roman Empire was suffering barbarian invasions. In 410 the Goths captured Rome, and the city was plundered by the Vandals in 455. The great Roman civilization had slowly crumbled away. The scholars who had traveled with the traders' caravans now stayed at home, and the interchange of ideas and scientific knowledge between the two worlds dwindled. Western science had suffered a crushing set-back.

To the east, however, remained the great civilizations of China and India. Here there was no such break in learning.

The science of the East
The civilization of China, founded on the banks of the Yellow River, was now about 2000 years old. Early Chinese civilization was based on agriculture and so the calendar was important. They took

Above: In 410 AD Rome was sacked. The great Roman Empire had provided conditions under which science flourished, but when it was overrun by the barbarians its cities were burned, its libraries destroyed. Below left: Long before the telescope, ancient astronomers were able to make astonishingly accurate observations of the heavens. Eastern scientists used great transits, built of masonry, to observe the stars and determine the key points in their calendars. Below: A Chinese water clock dating from the 11th century.

ALGEBRA

The Arabic word *al-jabr* (to reunite) gives us our word algebra. This is a branch of mathematics which includes the same operations as arithmetic (addition, multiplication, etc.), but uses symbols instead of numbers. The symbols enable mathematicians to form laws about how numbers behave.

The ancient Greeks invented geometric algebra, and made use of the fact that many mathematical relationships can be shown in diagrams. So, a^2 is the area of a square whose side is a units long. In the 9th century AD, the Arabs introduced symbols which could be used as known numbers are used. In this way they increased the scope of mathematics.

an intense interest in the heavens and had mapped nearly 1500 stars by the 4th century BC; they listed eclipses, comets, and meteors. They were also skilled mathematicians and doctors. But Chinese science, like the rest of Chinese culture, remained almost completely cut off from the West.

Indian science, too, placed great emphasis on astronomy and medicine. But unlike that of China it made an important contribution to the Western world. For it was in India that the decimal system and the use of nine figures and a zero were developed.

Islamic contributions

In the 7th century AD the successors of the Arab Muhammad, the founder of Islam, built up an empire which was to stretch from Spain to India. Muhammad's followers, the Muslims, eagerly pursued his instruction "to seek knowledge from the cradle to the grave". About the middle of the 9th century the Arabs adopted the Indian number system and the use of what are commonly called Arabic numerals. These made calculations much easier than the old systems such as the Roman, with its use of letters for numerals. The Arabs were very skilled mathematicians.

The Muslims turned five times a day to pray in the direction of Mecca. To do this they had to work out from the stars the direction in which Mecca lay, and several great observatories were built for this purpose. They were keen astronomers, and their major book of reference was the *Almagest*. This was in fact the Arab name for the astronomical work by Ptolemy of Alexandria.

As the Western countries became civilized once more, they became increasingly interested in Arab learning. Works on astronomy were among the books translated from Arabic to Latin. So knowledge based on the long-forgotten work of the Greeks, in many cases improved and expanded by the Arabs, took hold once more in Europe.

Above: According to tradition the Chinese knew in the 3rd millenium that a lodestone points to the magnetic north or south, and by about 800 AD were using it for navigation. This Italian miner's compass dates from the 1600s. Below: Arab astronomers.

The Alchemists

The alchemists' attempts to turn base metals into gold were doomed to failure. But their experiments were not entirely wasted – their observations and methods laid the groundwork for modern chemistry.

Above: This painting by Joseph Wright shows the German alchemist Hennig Brand in his laboratory, bathed in the light of the element phosphorus which he discovered in 1669. Alchemy formed the basis for modern chemistry.

Earth, air, fire, and water: these, Aristotle stated, were the four elements from which all substances were made up. The differences between substances were caused simply by the different proportions of elements. So it was not very extraordinary for people to think that they could alter one substance into another. All they had to do was find out just how they could alter the proportions of elements. And if they could change soft, gray lead into gold, then the result would be immense wealth and power.

Flasks and furnaces

The people who sought to alter substances were known as alchemists. They probably started work in the Egyptian city of Alexandria at about the time when Christ was born. Their "science" was an extraordinary mixture of practical experiments and mystical ideas. The flasks and furnaces they designed were decorated with secret symbols and they invented relationships between the metals and the stars.

One of the alchemists' great goals was to find the "philosopher's stone", a substance which would change any metal into gold. They also sought the *magisterium* which would cure all diseases. If they could only discover this, they thought, it would be but a small step to the elixir of life, by which a man could prolong his life for as long as he wished. In their experiments they combined and distilled all manner of substances and gained considerable knowledge of chemical reactions.

JABIR AND GEBER

Some 2000 early books on mystical subjects including alchemy are attributed to an Arab alchemist, Jabir ibn Hayyan, who is thought to have lived in the 8th century AD. Whether or not Jabir wrote all the books is not known, but the works strongly influenced alchemists who read them. The mysterious Jabir gained such a reputation that a 14th century Spanish alchemist adopted the westernized form of the name, Geber. Geber's own four books gave a clear description of the aims and methods of alchemy.

A design for a perpetual motion device – one that would move for ever without energy from outside. No one has yet invented such a machine.

THE QUEST FOR PERPETUAL MOTION

At the same time that alchemists in the Middle Ages were seeking to turn base metals into gold, other men were trying to perfect a machine which, once started, would continue working for ever without using any power.

There have been many attempts to construct a perpetual motion machine. None has been successful. From the quest for this machine, the law of conservation of energy was born. This states that energy cannot be created or destroyed, it can only be changed in form. The law rules out the possibility of perpetual motion because the energy which is unavoidably lost through friction must be replaced by an outside source of power.

Roger Bacon was accused of black magic, and confined for ten years by his Franciscan order because of his writings.

An alchemical tree, showing some of the strange symbols. The alchemists were very secret in their search for the philosopher's stone, writing in code and jealously guarding their findings.

From alchemy to science

Alchemy flourished in Europe and the Arab world. Many alchemists were quacks and charlatans, always ready to cheat the public. But others were serious men of science. Among these was Roger Bacon (?1220–1294). He was interested not only in alchemy and astronomy but also in mathematics and optics. Although Bacon was an alchemist, he went about his experiments in a very modern way. He believed that truth is found by observing how things behave. He described what may have been a kind of microscope and showed how lenses could make objects appear nearer. He constructed a kind of primitive steam engine and even foretold of a time when ships and carriages would be driven by engines.

The search for the philosopher's stone and the elixir of life was in vain, but the knowledge of chemistry that they had gained proved most valuable to future generations.

The World Reborn

As Europe emerged from the Middle Ages, a new spirit of enquiry inspired the arts and sciences. A genius of the period was Leonardo da Vinci, who did brilliant work in both fields.

Above: A self-portrait by Leonardo da Vinci (1452–1519). Possibly the greatest man of the Renaissance, he was both a brilliant painter and a scientific genius.

Below: Saint Peter's basilica in Rome is an example of the Renaissance throwback to classical architecture. The dome, for example, is built to precise mathematical proportions – typical of Greek and Roman building.

The word *renaissance* means re-birth; as used today it generally refers to the revival of learning that started in Italy in about the 14th century and spread all over Europe. Artists began to work directly from nature and to study mathematical proportion, as had their Greek and Roman forebears. With the Renaissance in the arts came the Renaissance of science.

An age of enterprise
At the same time, the way people lived was changing. The old feudal system was dying out and a new class of traders and artisans, living in towns and respecting intelligence and enterprise rather than birth, was growing. These people were behind the rapid development of technology in this period, as they searched for more efficient ways to manufacture goods. The rise of great mining families in northern Europe meant advances in assaying – the art of analysing ores and mixtures of metals – which laid some of the foundations of the science of chemistry. Another invention which had an important indirect effect on science was printing with movable type; this was essential to the spread of ideas from one country to another. One of the greatest men of the scientific Renaissance, who embodied both its questioning spirit and its inventiveness, was an Italian artist, Leonardo da Vinci. Leonardo, born in 1452, was not simply an artist who was interested in science; both ways of

thinking were united in his character. His notebooks contain drawings of countless projects and their explanations, set down in mirror writing for secrecy. They range over such subjects as anatomy, civil and military engineering, flight, and the movement of water. Again and again the links between the artist and the scientist can be seen. Leonardo's paintings show his interest in effects of light and colour; his notebooks record his scientific studies of light. The study of light led him on to study the eye itself. Another scientific study that arose from the artist's practical needs was anatomy; in this Leonardo was a pioneer. He was one of the first people to dissect human corpses to learn about the structure of the body under the skin.

Below: The Flemish city of Bruges in the 15th century. Increased trade led to the introduction of machines – with their extra efficiency and speed.

He left hundreds of accurate drawings of such things as the construction of the brain and the growth of an unborn child in the womb.

Leonardo the prophet

Leonardo's talent for drawing was extraordinary – he could capture the most minute and fleeting details on paper. He even made a series of drawings of water in motion, which was the only record of the subject until the invention of high-speed photography.

Leonardo also employed his talents in the design of machines. He is credited with many lasting inventions, such as pointed bullets, the paddle wheel for boats, and the mincing machine. But it is as a prophet of modern technology that Leonardo the scientist is best remembered today. He anticipated such modern ideas as the tank and the parachute; and he was fascinated by the idea of a flying machine. He explored ways of flying helped by currents of air. But the wings of his aircraft are all based on careful study of the wings of birds and bats. None of these machines would have flown if ever built.

Leonardo left many of his paintings and other objects unfinished – frustrated, it seems, by the impossibility of reaching absolute perfection. The world in the Renaissance was already too complex for one mind.

Above: Leonardo was the first man to design a helicopter. In this he was centuries ahead of his time – the first manned helicopter did not fly until the early 20th century.

Right: A striking example of the fusion of Leonardo's artistic and scientific abilities. His anatomical drawings were extremely accurate and easily surpassed the work of his contempories.

Below: One of Leonardo's many flight machines.

A New Look at the Universe

Copernicus' statement that the Earth moved around the Sun was denied by the Church authorities. But he was right – and his "heresy" proved the key to the understanding of the universe.

Above: Nicolaus Copernicus (1473–1543), who established that the Sun, and not the Earth, was the center of the universe.

Right: Galileo with the telescopes he used to observe the Sun and planets.

In 1492 Columbus landed in the Americas. By sailing west he had reached what he thought was the East; and the idea that the Earth was round gained in popularity. Among the people whose imagination was fired by Columbus's voyage was a 19-year-old student from Cracow in Poland, Nicolaus Copernicus (1473–1543).

Copernicus had come across a theory put forward by Aristarchus nearly 18 centuries earlier but long discarded: that the Sun was the center of the universe.

Like many Renaissance scientists,

Below: The Solar System as seen by Copernicus.

Above: Johannes Kepler (1571–1630) proved that planets orbit in ellipses rather than circles.

Below: Issac Newton (1642–1727), one of the most brilliant of all scientists.

Copernicus was wealthy enough to pursue a life of study. By 1536 he had almost finished his great work, *Concerning the Revolution of the Heavenly Spheres*; but it was not published until the year of his death in 1543. In it Copernicus maintained that the Sun was the center of the universe and that the Earth was only one of the planets that revolve around the Sun.

Planetary motion

Johannes Kepler was born in 1571. It was Kepler who found that planetary orbits are ellipses, rather than circles, as Copernicus had thought, and it was Kepler who expressed the laws of planetary motion, which paved the way for the work of Sir Isaac Newton.

Roughly contemporary with Kepler was the brilliant scientist, Galileo Galilei. He challenged Aristotle's teaching that heavy bodies fall faster than light ones. Galileo reasoned that the force of gravity pulls all bodies to Earth with the same acceleration, regardless of their weight.

In 1609 Galileo built his own telescope and began observing the planets and stars. He became convinced that Copernicus' Sun-centered theory of the universe was correct. The Church bitterly opposed his theory that it was the Earth that moved around the Sun and he was ordered to recant. The story goes that having done this. Galileo added under his breath, *'E pur si muove'* ('Yet it *does* move').

A universal force

Sir Isaac Newton was born in 1642. He was a mathematician, astronomer, physicist, and a man who thought deeply about all that he observed around him.

As a young man, Newton mastered the science of mathematics. Before his 30th birthday he had conducted many experiments to determine the nature of light, and invented the type of reflecting telescope that bears his name.

Newton recognized that there was a force that extended throughout the universe, and controlled the stars in their courses as much as it did the fall of an apple from a tree – the universal force of gravitation. He showed that the gravitational force of the Sun keeps the planets in their orbits. Newton's laws of gravitation and motion were published in 1687. It was the first book to set out a unified system of scientific principles explaining how the universe is held together, and it became the bible of physicists for nearly two centuries.

Above: A modern 41-inch reflecting telescope, at Yerkes Observatory.

Below: One story has it that Galileo proved that all objects fall with the same acceleration by dropping two different weights from the top of Pisa's Leaning Tower.

Rembrandt painted "The Anatomy Lesson" in 1632. For a long time the Church had strongly opposed the dissection of corpses, and the early anatomists had often been forced to carry out dissection in secret. But the tide of the Renaissance was too strong, and by the mid 17th century anatomy was an accepted study.

Below: Vesalius with his anatomical models. Vesalius first learned anatomy by dissecting the bodies of dead criminals. As well as attempting to standardize anatomical terms his works set a new standard of clear and even beautiful medical illustration.

The Anatomists

The Church authorities had rejected Copernicus's vision of a Sun-centered universe. Vesalius and Harvey faced similar religious opposition as they fought to disprove many of the prevaling ideas about the human body.

In the 2nd century AD, Claudius Galenus, better known as Galen, a physician from Pergamum (now Bergama, in Turkey), discovered that arteries contained blood and not air as some Greek physicians had taught. He also knew that in some way the heart made the blood move, but he did not understand how it circulated. Galen believed that blood behaved like the tides, reaching all parts of the body with a gentle ebb and flow.

The founder of modern anatomy
This theory, and the belief that different parts of the human body were controlled by different stars, were widely accepted until the time of Andreas Vesalius, an anatomist born in Brussels in 1514. Vesalius was the founder of modern anatomy. In 1538 he published an attempt to standardize anatomical terms. His most important work came later in 1543, when, following numerous dissections, he published *De Humani Corporis Fabrica*, the first complete

description of human anatomy. Galen's supporters angrily reproached Vesalius for contradicting Galen's theory of the movement of blood, although Vesalius had not proposed his own theory.

In 1564 Vesalius was condemned to death by the Church authorities – either

Above: A drawing from Harvey's great work on the circulation of blood, published in 1628. Scientists sometimes employed artists to draw illustrations for them.

for stealing bodies from graves and dissecting them, or for carrying out a post mortem on a man whose heart was still beating. The sentence was commuted to a pilgrimage of penance to Jerusalem, but Vesalius died on the return journey at the age of 50.

Understanding the heart
But mystery still surrounded the action of the heart. The English physician, William Harvey, provided the solution.

Harvey was born at Folkestone, England, in 1578. At the age of 16 he went to Caius College in Cambridge to study medicine. Then he attended lectures in Padua given by Galileo at a time when the great Italian was investigating the mechanics of the pump. It may be that Harvey was influenced by Galileo's work, for he later likened the action of the heart to that of a pump.

On his return to England, Harvey continued his work on the movements of the heart and blood. He measured the amount of blood which the heart pumped at a single beat. He found that the blood moved away from the heart in arteries and towards it in veins. The remaining question was how the blood passed from the arteries to the veins. Harvey guessed at the presence of capillaries – tiny blood vessels which connect the smallest veins and arteries. All his theories were gathered together in one of the most important works in the history of physiology, *An Anatomical Treatise on the Movement of the Heart and Blood in Animals*, published in 1628. Harvey lived to see his theories accepted by eminent anatomists all over Europe, where he was known and honored.

Despite strong opposition from the Church, which regarded dissections as a violation of the human body, Vesalius and Harvey had radically changed people's ideas about the human body.

Above: A drawing by Vesalius showing the major muscles of the human body.

Above: William Harvey (1578–1657) proved that blood circulated around the body and thought of the heart as a pump.

Left: Our knowledge of human anatomy is such that we can now build machines that serve as parts of the body. This heart/lung machine functions as the heart and lungs during an operation. Without such machines it would not be possible to perform certain types of surgery.

Invisible Elements

The pioneer chemists of the 17th and 18th centuries were fascinated by the most familiar but intangible of substances – air.

Above: Boyle's Law. If the pressure on a gas is doubled, its compressed molecules (represented here by lines) occupy half the space.

In the 17th century, air was losing its mystery. The invention of the air pump enabled Robert Boyle, an Irish chemist, to investigate the properties of gases. In 1662 he published what is now known as Boyle's Law, which says that the volume of a gas at a constant temperature varies inversely with the pressure upon it.

In the same year Boyle made another important discovery. While working in his laboratory he noticed that a candle burning in an enclosed space went out before all the air has been used up. He knew that air consists of two parts, one which supports combustion and one which does not.

Left: Charts of the elements and their atomic weights and models of atoms, used by John Dalton in his lectures.

JOHN DALTON 1766–1844 first introduced the idea that all compounds consist of molecules containing elements in a fixed proportion.

Phlogiston

The German chemist, Georg Ernst Stahl, put forward a theory of the burning process in 1697. He claimed that all inflammable materials contained "phlostigon" and that this was given off when they burned. His theory seemed to reinforce Boyle's beliefs about air, since combustion would stop when all the phlostigon in a substance was given off, though air might still be present.

Most scientists seemed to regard all gases as some form of air. Henry Cavendish discovered "inflammable air" in 1766. We now know it as hydrogen.

Joseph Priestley, an English chemist, did not share this belief that all gases were a form of air. He discovered carbon monoxide, hydrochloric acid gas, and sulfur dioxide. In 1772 Priestley and Daniel Rutherford independently discovered nitrogen, the gas which makes up 78 per cent of the air. But in 1774 Priestley made by far his most important discovery. He obtained a new gas which appeared to support combustion far better than ordinary air. He noticed that mice became very frisky when breathing this gas. Priestley had discovered oxygen. The part that oxygen plays in combustion was first understood by Antoine Lavoisier, a French chemist.

The secret of burning

Antoine Laurent Lavoisier was, with Robert Boyle, the founder of modern chemistry. He correctly explained combustion as a combination of the burning substance with Priestley's new gas, which he now termed oxygen. Lavoisier's experiments led him to formulate, in 1789, the law of conservation of matter, which states that matter can be neither created nor destroyed.

Lavoisier remains one of the greatest brains of the 18th century. He was guillotined in 1794 during the French

Revolution on a petty accusation.

Air and other substances had now been broken down into their constituent elements. It remained for John Dalton, an English chemist, to show how the parts were bonded together.

John Dalton discovered that when two gases combine they always do so in fixed proportions. Dalton's famous atomic theory stated that an element consists of identical atoms and that these combine in simple proportions to form chemical compounds. His principles have been accepted as the basis of modern atomic theory.

ROBERT BOYLE 1627–1691 (top left) was a founder-member of the Royal Society in London.

JOSEPH PRIESTLEY 1733–1804 (right) is best remembered for his discovery of several gases, notably oxygen.

ANTOINE LAURENT LAVOISIER 1743–1794 (right) published what was perhaps the first modern chemistry book.

Below: Priestley works on the problem of combustion.

The Ladder of Life

Above: The biblical story of creation was believed to be true until the middle of the 19th century.

When it became clear that the Earth was not the center of the universe, scientists began to question the unique place of Man in the scheme of creation.

Men of all religions and creeds had always believed in the theory of "individual creation" – that all living things had been created separately and individually by some divine being, whatever name was given to him. Man was the creator's greatest achievement.

When work began on the science of comparative anatomy – comparing the ways in which different creatures were constructed – this belief was shaken. In the 18th century men like the Scottish anatomist John Hunter pointed out such disturbing facts as the resemblance of the embryos of higher animals like Man to the adult forms of lower ones such as fish. He also showed that the embryo of a mammal begins to look like a mammal only towards the end of its growth. Could the theory of individual creation be wrong?

"The Ladder of Nature"

When the Swedish naturalist, Carolus Linnaeus (1707–1778) introduced his system of classifying plants and animals, He called Man "a master animal". In his system, still used today, each living thing has a two-part Latin name: the first is the *genus* (group) and the second is the *species* (kind). For example, the dog-rose is *Rosa canina*. Linnaeus believed that his classification of the natural world applied to all periods of time. While claiming that "Man is the only creature that God has created with an immortal soul", he had to admit that he found it difficult "to discover one attribute by which Man can be distinguished from apes. . . ."

The French naturalist, Georges Cuvier (1769–1832), who also believed in individual creation, classified the animal world with such completeness that he could virtually identify an animal from a mere fragment.

At about the time Cuvier was producing his systematic work, the Chevalier de Lamarck (1744–1829), was putting forward sensational theories on the development of species. He visualized a "ladder of nature", in which each species had been changed into another, and the extinct ones had given rise to those now living. In a more limited way, this had already been appreciated by Erasmus Darwin (1731–1802), grand-

---

SEVERINO 1580–1656
Pioneer of comparative anatomy.

GEORGES CUVIER 1769–1832
French naturalist. Produced the first complete classification of the animal kingdom.

JOHN HUNTER 1728–1793
Noticed that the embryos of mammals pass through stages of resemblance to lower animals.

ERASMUS DARWIN 1731–1802
Grandfather of Charles Darwin. Anticipated Lamarck's theory of evolution by understanding the mechanics of selective breeding.

CHARLES DARWIN 1809–1882
Great English naturalist. Proposed the theory of natural selection, the first theory of evolution.

GREGOR MENDEL 1822–1884
Austrian botanist who formulated the laws of heredity through his breeding experiments with peas.

ather of the great Charles Darwin. He realized that the farming practice of selective breeding improved the quality of farm stock through controlling the inheritance of the best characteristics of the species.

Voyage on the "Beagle"

Charles Darwin (1809–1882), was the first person to put forward a sound theory of evolution backed by observation. As a young naturalist on a five-year-long survey of the South Atlantic and Pacific Oceans aboard the *Beagle*, Darwin's ideas took shape. He noticed that the giant tortoises of the Galapagos Islands differed slightly from one island to another. Environment, he concluded, had put its mark on each separate genetic line. The same was true of the birds he found there. In 1859 he startled the world with the publication of his famous book, *The Origin of Species*, in which he set out his theories of natural selection, or the "survival of the fittest".

Darwin stated that if an individual happens to have different characteristics from its relatives, and if these characteristics enable it to survive more easily, it will thrive, while the others will die out. In this way a superior species will evolve.

The secret of heredity

An Austrian monk named Gregor Mendel (1822–1884) formulated the laws of heredity, or how characteristics are passed from parents to children. This was in 1864, following a series of experiments on the cross-breeding of peas. What he had discovered was the existence of genes, which carry information from one generation to the next.

In 1831, Charles Darwin was appointed naturalist to HMS "Beagle", a survey ship due to make a voyage around the world. In the Galapagos Islands he noticed how the tortoises (left) and finches (right) differed from island to island. He realized that this was due to the different environments in which they lived.

Trofim Lysenko, born in Russia in 1898. In 1928 he made a series of claims that contradicted Mendel's views on genetics. He stated that a plant's characteristics could be changed by grafting. He was supported by Joseph Stalin and his views were enforced on Soviet scientists.

In 1857 Mendel began to experiment with garden peas. He cross-bred green (g) peas with yellow (Y) peas and the next generation peas were all yellow. But when these peas were cross-bred in turn, they always produced one green pea for every three yellow. Mendel concluded that the first generation of peas carried the traits of both parents, but that the Y trait over-ruled the g trait.

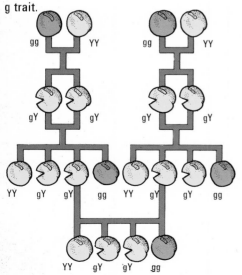

gg   YY   gg   YY

gY   gY   gY   gY

YY gY gY gg   YY gY gY gg

YY gY gY gg

Tools of the Scientist

Through the ages, scientists have demanded precise tools and instruments to examine, measure, and record natural phenomena.

Above: An Egyptian balance, a reasonably accurate measure for grain and other dry goods.

Above: A 16th-century print depicting the Greek scientist Ptolemy, guided by the Muse of Astronomy, using a quadrant to measure the altitude of the Moon.

The scientist's need for tools to detect and measure things i reflected in the early appearance of the telescope, the microscop and other devices. Man has always used tools to help him in hi work. A scientist's tools differ from others in their precision. Th Egyptian pyramids and Stonehenge, for example, could only hav been constructed so accurately with the aid of scientifi instruments to measure lengths and angles.

The 17th century was the great period of invention. One of th first telescopes was made by the Dutchman Hans Lippershey i 1608, when comparing two spectacle lenses, one behind the othe The telescope enabled men to view the heavenly bodies with muc more accuracy.

A whole new world of study was opened to scientists by th invention of the microscope by another Dutchman, Zacharia Janssen, in 1590, although it was not widely used until Robe Hooke developed it in the 1660s. Now hitherto invisible objects the hairs on an insect's leg, the cells in a leaf – could be studied

The chronometer, a very accurate time-keeping device, was fir constructed by an Englishman, John Harrison, in the 18th century This instrument enabled men to plot accurately their course at se

The huge atomic particle accelerator which scientists use toda may be a far cry from the simple Egyptian balance, but both wer invented as tools to help the scientist to observe and record fact and build up a picture of the universe.

Left: The vacuum pump, first developed in the 17th century, was used by Otto von Guericke and Robert Boyle in their early experiments with air.

Right: An early electrical machine. These simple devices were used for producing electricity in the laboratory in order to carry out experiments in electromagnetism.

Above: An analytical balance patented by F. Sartorius in 1870. It can detect a difference in weight of one-tenth of a milligram.
Below: "The Orrery" by Joseph Wright. These working models of the planets in the Solar System were very popular in the 18th and 19th centuries.

Above: A microscope belonging to Robert Hooke, whose great work "Micrographia" (1665) described the structure of plant and animal cells.

Above: A modern electron microscope. In 1926 Hans Busch discovered that electrons could be used instead of light rays to achieve a much greater magnifying power. Modern electron microscopes can magnify up to a million times and have made possible tremendous advances in research.

Reading the Rocks

Above: Mary Anning (1799–1847). Aged 11 she discovered the first ichthyosaur fossil and a few years later the first complete plesiosaur.

Below: "Dinner is served"... in the Iguanodon. A stage in the reconstruction of a dinosaur, in 1854.

Fossils in the rocks were long explained by the Biblical flood. Scientific study of extinct creatures, begun in the 18th century, soon became a fashionable pursuit.

In 1854 the Crystal Palace, home of the Great Exhibition of 1851, was moved from its original site in Hyde Park, London, to Sydenham in south London. Victorian sightseers were then treated to a display of life-size models of dinosaurs and other extinct animals, placed among the trees and shrubbery of the Crystal Palace grounds. The study and collecting of fossils had become a "fashionable science".

Before the Flood
Since before the time of the ancient Greeks, men had known about fossils and observed their similarity to some living sea creatures. In Renaissance times the accepted explanation was that Noah's flood had covered the continents, and that when the waters had receded, these creatures had been stranded and died.

Two men, both born in 1769, can be credited as the first to read the world's history from its rocks: the French naturalist Baron Georges Cuvier, and William Smith, an English geologist. Cuvier applied to extinct creatures his methods of classification of living animals, using anatomical details rather than external appearances. This made it easier to relate extinct animals to one another as well as to their modern descendants.

While Cuvier enjoyed the best of educations, William Smith, son of a blacksmith, was entirely self taught. None the less he made the first geological maps, and pointed out that particular fossils always occur in the same layers of the Earth's crust. For the first time these layers could be dated, since scientists

Below: A nest of dinosaur eggs, belonging to a Protoceratops.
Bottom: Edward Cope (1840–1897), a great fossil hunter whose spectacular finds helped to make paleontology a popular science.

knew when the fossilized animals in them had lived. Smith had provided later workers with what has been called "the key to all geological research".

In the 19th century the infant science of paleontology – the science of the study of fossils – grew in popularity. This was largely due to the work of men like the English paleontologist Gideon Mantell, and Richard Owen, an English anatomist. Mantell found the remains of the dinosaur *Iguanodon*, a 15-foot-high reptile, in Sussex, England in 1822. Richard Owen analysed *Iguanodon*, *Megalosaurus*, and *Hylaeosaurus*, and concluded that they were not the ancestors of modern lizards, but belonged to an extinct sub-order, which he named *Dinosauria* (from the Greek *deinos*, meaning terrible, and *sauros*, meaning lizard).

American finds
The really spectacular fossil finds of the 19th century came from central and western America. In 1871 Edward Cope, an American naturalist, set out to find and describe all the extinct fishes, reptiles, and mammals of the western USA, from Texas to Wyoming. At times, threatened by hostile Indians, he had to collect his fossils with a rifle in one hand. Cope was one of the first to realize that the really important work begins after the

fossil has been found, when it must be identified and classified.

Cope's great rival was Othniel Marsh, a paleontologist. A race developed between the two men to find the first fossil dinosaurs. Marsh was aided in his searches by the financial backing of his uncle, George Peabody, who built the Peabody Museum of Natural History at Yale to house Marsh's finds. The enmity between Marsh and Cope had its advantages. Between them they managed to find and identify more than 130 species of dinosaurs, including *Brontosaurus*, *Diplodocus*, and *Hadrosaurus*. A huge mass of specimens was accumulated.

The earliest fossil remains of men were not recognized as such. Only after Darwin and his followers had gained acceptance for the idea that Man was descended from ape-like creatures did the search for the fossil remains of his ancestors become widespread. The paleontologists traveled to Java, Peking, and Africa to piece together the history of Man's evolution.

Above: The skeleton of a dinosaur under reconstruction. There were often only isolated bones to work from and the overall shape of the dinosaur had to be guessed at.

Above: Othniel Marsh (1831–1899). His bitter race against Edward Cope to discover the first fossil dinosaurs led to the discovery of many specimens.

A New Form of Energy

William Gilbert finally disproved the belief that magnetism and electricity were forms of magic. His work raised them to a level worthy of serious scientific study.

Electricity and magnetism have been known to Man, in their natural forms, for thousands of years. In about 600 BC the Greeks found that amber attracted feathers and other light objects when rubbed vigorously. Lodestone, a natural ore, was found to attract pieces of iron, and compasses were probably used as early as AD 700. But such properties were generally regarded as magical.

William Gilbert (1540–1603), an English physicist and court physician to Elizabeth I, took a more scientific approach. He studied magnets and compasses and put forward a theory, published in 1600, that the Earth is a huge magnet, and that this explains the direction of magnetic north and the dipping of the magnetic needle in a compass.

First electric machines
In 1672 Otto von Guericke (1602–1686), mayor of Magdeburg, constructed a machine which could produce electricity in greater quantities than had been possible before. His machine was simply a ball of sulfur which rotated at great speed. When Guericke rubbed his hand against the spinning ball, an electric charge was induced in it, and it would attract light objects. At greater speeds the ball sparked. This was the first clue to the

Above: Benjamin Franklin demonstrated the electrical nature of lightning by flying a kite in a thunderstorm and drawing sparks from a key.

The Leyden jar was invented in 1746 to store electricity. The jar is coated with tinfoil. Charges are passed down the brass rod to the tinfoil in which they are stored.

Above: Humphry Davy (1778–1829), a brilliant English chemist. He is chiefly remembered for inventing the miner's safety lamp, named after him, but he made many other contributions to 19th-century science. By inhaling nitrous oxide he discovered its anesthetic properties. He was also the first to isolate the elements sodium, potassium, barium, magnesium, and strontium.

Below: Otto von Guericke's static electricity generator, invented in 1672. Guericke's other main contribution to science was the invention of the air pump in 1650.

similarity between electricity and lightning. It was another 80 years before this link was established by Benjamin Franklin (1706–1790).

Franklin's kite

Franklin believed that lightning was a discharge of electricity from the atmosphere to the Earth. To test his theory he performed a dangerous experiment. During a thunderstorm he flew a kite with a metal key on the end of a string. At the tip of the kite was a metal spike. Electricity passed from the atmosphere into the spike and down the wet string to the key where a spark appeared. Franklin had proved the existence of electricity in the cloud. This experiment led Franklin to invent the lightning conductor.

Further progress in electrical science was hampered by the lack of a steady supply of electricity. The Leyden jar, invented in 1746 in Leyden, Holland, could store static electricity. Franklin gave the jar its characteristic form, coating it with tin foil. But the Leyden jar could not produce a steady current.

The voltaic pile

An important breakthrough was made in 1800, when Alessandro Volta (1745–1827), an Italian physicist, constructed the first electric battery. The basic unit of the "voltaic pile" was a piece of zinc and a piece of copper separated by a fabric pad soaked in a dilute acid. This produced a current, flowing from one metal to the other, and by building a "pile" of these units, he could intensify the flow of current. Scientists now had a manageable source of current which they could use in their experiments.

Another experimenter of the time who had great success in his work with Volta's pile was Humphry Davy (1778–1829). One of his most important experiments was the decomposition of molten soda into the metal sodium and water, by passing an electric current through it – a process known as electrolysis. A similar experiment yielded the element potassium.

Davy was a brilliant chemist and famous as an eloquent lecturer. Although best remembered as the inventor of the miner's safety lamp and the discoverer of the anesthetic properties of nitrous oxide (laughing gas), his greatest contribution to science was his work on the electrical nature of chemical bonds.

ANIMAL ELECTRICITY
Luigi Galvani (1737–1798), professor of anatomy at Bologna, spent 11 years studying the effect of electricity on the nerves and muscles of animals. Many of his experiments involved passing electric currents through frogs' legs, which would twitch as the muscle contracted. In 1786 he noticed that if the nerve in a pair of legs was connected to a copper rod and the muscle to an iron one, and the two metals were also in contact, the legs would twitch although he had not applied any current.

Galvani concluded that "animal electricity" was being produced. He was mistaken; the electric current was produced by the chemical action of very weak acids in the legs on the two metals, which, being in contact, formed a complete circuit.

MICHAEL FARADAY 1791–1867, the son of a blacksmith, laid the basis of electro-chemistry and of modern electronic sciences.

JAMES CLERK MAXWELL 1831–1879 used a mathematical description to support Faraday's discovery of electromagnetism. He showed that light itself is electro-magnetic and predicted the existence of other electromagnetic waves.

HERMANN HELMHOLTZ 1821-1894, a German physicist, is noted for his contributions to optics, acoustics, and electromagnetism.

HEINRICH HERTZ 1857–1894 was born in Hamburg and trained first as an engineer. As a physicist, he is famous for his experiment with Hertzian or electro-magnetic waves.

Towards Wireless Waves

Michael Faraday demonstrated the link between magnetism and electricity. The way was open for other scientists to put electricity to work.

The work of Faraday and others in the 19th century led to a clearer understanding of the link between electricity and magnetism. In 1820 the Danish physicist and chemist, Hans Christian Oersted, noticed, while lecturing in Paris, that when he passed an electric current through a conductor it made a nearby magnetic needle deflect. He had stumbled across the link between electricity and magnetism. Within a few weeks the French scientist André-Marie Ampère had shown that when a current is passed through a wire it produces a magnetic field.

Generating electricity

Oersted and Ampère had shown that a magnetic field could be created by an electric current. Michael Faraday, an English chemist and physicist, was to show that the reverse was possible too. Faraday was born in London in 1791. At the age of 12 he took a job in a bookshop. He had time to read many books, and became interested in the new science of electricity. In 1812 he sent the eminent chemist, Sir Humphry Davy, notes of Davy's own lectures at the Royal Institution. Davy was impressed and offered Faraday a job as his laboratory assistant.

In 1831 Faraday performed two important experiments. In the first, he showed that an alternating current in one conductor will induce a current in a second nearby conductor, although there is no electrical connection between them. In the second, he demonstrated that when a magnet is moved in and out of a coil of wire, a current is created in the coil. Faraday had discovered two ways of generating electricity. The dynamos and electric motors later invented were a direct result of his discoveries.

One of Faraday's most important feats was to establish the laws of electrolysis – bringing about a chemical reaction by passing an electric current through a solution. One application of electrolysis is in electroplating. Below, a spoon is coated with chromium from a solution of chromic acid through which a current is passed.

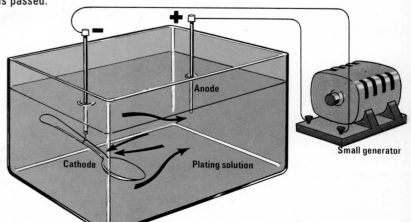

Electromagnetic waves

Nearly 30 years after Faraday's discoveries James Clerk Maxwell (1831–1879), a Scottish physicist, used Faraday's experimental results to produce equations which showed the precise relationship between electricity and magnetism. He believed that a vibrating electric charge would produce electromagnetic waves (waves which have both electric and magnetic properties). He calculated their velocity and saw that it was the same as the speed of light. From this he correctly concluded that light itself was a form of electromagnetic wave. Maxwell only guessed at the existence of these waves. A German physicist, Heinrich Hertz (1857–1894), was to prove it.

Hertz initially trained as an engineer, but he became interested in physics and learned much as the student of another great German scientist, Hermann Helmholtz. Helmholtz realized the need for a test of Maxwell's theory, and he made it the subject of a competition for students. His brilliant pupil Hertz successfully performed the test in 1888 and proved the existence of electromagnetic (or Hertzian) waves. Hertz found that they had identical properties to those of light and heat waves. It was becoming clear that there was a whole spectrum of electromagnetic waves – the visible spectrum of light, and the invisible spectrum ranging from gamma rays to the ultra-violet, and infra-red to radio waves. Hertz had conclusively established the existence and form of electromagnetic waves, and prepared the ground for the development of radio.

The world's first generating station was opened by Thomas Edison in New York in September 1882. The Deptford power station, London (right), was opened in 1889.

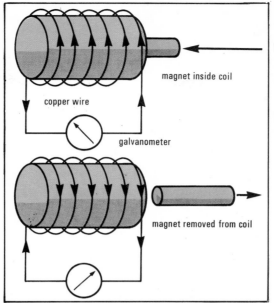

Faraday demonstrated that when a magnet is moved in and out of a coil a current is created. Current flows one way when the magnet is moved in, and the other way when it is moved out.

Above: Hertz's oscillator and resonator, which confirmed the existence of electromagnetic waves. A current produced in the induction coil causes a spark to jump across the gap between the terminals. Electromagnetic waves thus released set up a similar current and spark in the copper ring of the resonator.

Left: Two of the machines invented by James Wimshurst (1832–1903) for generating static electricity. When the handle is turned, the machine builds up a charge.

The Microbe Hunters

Through their work, Pasteur, Jenner, and Lister revolutionized medicine and gave Man a vital weapon in the war against disease.

In 1683 a Dutch draper, Anton van Leeuwenhoek, peered through a home-made microscope at a drop of canal water, and found it was seething with tiny creatures. He described these animalcules, as he called them, as being 1000 times smaller than the eye of a louse. He was the first to see the micro-organisms we call bacteria.

At that time it was commonly thought that the lower forms of life – including such things as weevils, protozoa, and even shellfish – could be produced by non-living matter. This process was known as spontaneous generation. The micro-organisms seen under the micro-scope also seemed to appear out of "nothing" – Leeuwenhoek saw clear broths produce increasing numbers of them as days went by. Leeuwenhoek did not believe they came from spontaneous

The first "vaccination" against smallpox was in 1796; by 1801 Edward Jenner reported that at least 100,000 people in Britain had been vaccinated. This cartoon by James Gillray mocks supposed effects of the cowpox germs.

Louis Pasteur proved the connection between micro-organisms and fermentation and disease. The inoculations he pioneered have saved the lives of countless millions of men and animals.

Pasteur inoculated patients with a weakened strain of a disease which prevented them from catching it thereafter. The forerunner of this practice was Edward Jenner (left), an English doctor who had immunized people against smallpox by inoculating them with the germs of cowpox, a similar but very much milder disease. Before this, smallpox was widespread, killing many people and leaving others hideously scarred.

generation; "We can now easily conceive," he wrote, "that . . . in all waters exposed to the air, animalcules may be found; for they may be carried thither by the particles of dust blown about by the winds." But it was two centuries before this theory was proved by the work of Louis Pasteur.

Louis Pasteur
Pasteur was born in 1822, the son of a tanner in southeast France. At the age of

EDWARD JENNER
In the 18th century, smallpox was still a scourge. Edward Jenner (1749–1823), a doctor in Gloucester-shire, England, became interested in the local belief that cowpox (a disease of cattle which sometimes infects the hands of milkers) made people immune to smallpox.

In 1796 Jenner put matter from cowpox sores into a cut on the arm of James Phipps, an 8-year-old boy. When the resulting cowpox sores had cleared up, Jenner infected him with smallpox. The boy remained healthy and Jenner's discovery was soon known throughout the medical world.

19 he decided to become a scientist and went to Paris to study. His first important work was on crystal structures; this led him on to wonder about the structures of living things and he began to investigate the simplest forms of life.

In 1854 Pasteur became professor and dean of the faculty of science at Lille. At that time local manufacturers of alcohol were suffering appalling losses through the souring of alcohol during the fermentation process. Pasteur turned his attention to fermentation in wine and beer. He found that the sour liquids contained micro-organisms which prevented proper fermentation. He went on

These bacteria (magnified × 740) fell from the air on to a coated plate. They are of different shapes and sizes; some are harmless, others can cause disease. Pasteur was the first to realize the effects of these invisible airborne hordes.

to show that micro-organisms also caused the souring of milk.

Where did these micro-organisms come from? Did they fall from the air, or were they generated in the liquids? Ever since Leeuwenhoek's day scientists had fought for these rival theories. Now Pasteur, in a series of experiments, showed that while a sterilized liquid protected from atmospheric dust would

In the 18th century surgical techniques were crude. By the mid-19th century techniques of surgery were greatly improved, but the death rate from wound infection was terrifyingly high.

Joseph Lister (1827–1912), influenced by Pasteur's work, founded antiseptic surgery.

Left: Pasteur's flask. The broth inside, boiled to kill any living things, did not decay, because the microbes in the air were trapped in the bent neck. When the neck was snapped off the broth decayed.

remain pure for months, micro-organisms were growing in it only a few hours after it was exposed to the open air.

Pasteur showed that not only fermentation but also the decomposition of organic matter was caused by certain micro-organisms, or "germs", in the air. He showed how these could be killed by heat, in the process called pasteurization named after him. His work came to the attention of a British surgeon called Joseph Lister, who realized that germs might be the cause of the wound infections which made surgical operations so dangerous. Lister could not use heat to kill the germs; he killed them instead by placing an antiseptic "barrier" of carbolic acid between the wound and the air. Deaths from wound infections dropped dramatically.

Pasteur found that animals injected with specially weakened strains of the bacteria which caused diseases suffered from only mild attacks of the diseases – and, far more important, they later proved immune to full-strength bacteria. Pasteur's last great success was in producing a vaccine to immunize people against the fatal and agonizing disease rabies, which they contracted by being bitten by an infected animal.

Linking the Continents

Samuel Morse (1791–1872), inventor of the electric telegraph. He also devised the Morse Code.

Scientists had proved the existence of electromagnetic waves which could be transmitted through the air without wires. Now they searched for a way to use these waves to transmit information – and then speech.

The first clue that electricity might be the key to rapid communications was provided in 1820 when Hans Oersted, a Danish physicist and chemist, discovered that an electric current could deflect a magnetic needle. The importance of his discovery was quickly appreciated by the German mathematician, Karl Gauss (1777–1855). He used different letters of the alphabet, so that as each letter was transmitted, a needle was deflected to a different position.

Messages by wire

From this idea came the first electric telegraph, built and demonstrated in 1837 by Samuel Morse (1791–1872), an American artist who became interested in electricity. A key at the sending end was used to produce long and short bursts of current – dots and dashes – in what became known as the Morse code. At the receiving end a pen was moved by an electromagnet to inscribe these dots and dashes on a moving band of paper. By the time Morse died, messages in Morse code were being carried to all parts of the world.

The chief drawback to the use of the Morse telegraph was that its operators had to be skilled in the use of his code. The ideal, the transmission of speech, seemed impossible until the work of Alexander Graham Bell (1847–1922) proved otherwise.

"Mr Watson, come here . . .!"

Bell did not know much about electricity, but he understood the human voice, for

The original Morse telegraph. Messages are sent by means of a Morse key and a sounder, connected to a low-voltage electric circuit. The sender makes long and short electric pulses with the key, which cause the sounder (an electromagnet) to click against an iron bar.

Alexander Graham Bell, inventor of the telephone, inaugurating the New York – Chicago line in October 1892.

he was professor of voice physiology at Boston University. He believed it was possible to transmit all the sounds of the human voice over a telegraph system. In June 1875, while experimenting with the help of his assistant, Thomas Watson, Bell heard a noise over his machine from the room where Watson was working. It was the first step towards a working telephone. In March 1876 the first intelligible sentence was transmitted over the telephone. Bell and Watson were about to try out a new transmitter when Bell cried: "Mr Watson, come here, I want you!" Bell had spilt some battery acid down his trousers. Watson, hearing Bell's cry on the receiver in the next room, rushed in triumph to Bell. Their invention was a success.

The next step forward came with wireless communication. In 1888 the German Heinrich Hertz became the first to demonstrate the production and reception of electromagnetic waves. When Hertz discovered these waves, he thought that they would be of theoretical interest only, but in fact they paved the way for radio.

In 1890 the French physicist Edouard

Branly invented a receiver for electromagnetic waves, which he called a coherer. Four years later a Russian, Aleksander Popov, invented an antenna which improved the range over which electromagnetic waves could be transmitted. The way was open for the young Italian scientist, Guglielmo Marconi (1874–1937), to produce the first "wireless".

The first radio message

In 1894 Marconi used Hertzian waves and a coherer to make a bell ring at a distance of 15 feet from the source. By 1899 he had increased its range to 75 miles. Scientists thought that there would be a limit to the distance that radio messages could be sent. After all, radio waves travel in straight lines, and the Earth's surface is curved. At some point the signal would be lost in space. But in 1901, Marconi transmitted the Morse letter "S" from England to Newfoundland. The radio waves had been bent round the Earth by bouncing them off a layer in the upper atmosphere, called the ionosphere. Radio was now a reality.

From Marconi's first radio, our systems of communication have rapidly expanded. Television, and the ability of astronauts to talk to us from the Moon, now seem merely a matter of course.

Above: The inventor of radio, Guglielmo Marconi, with apparatus similar to that which he used to send the first wireless signal across the Atlantic – the Morse letter "S", transmitted from England to Newfoundland in 1901.

TELEVISION

The discovery of radio led, some 25 years later, to the development of television – a more complex instrument but based on the same principles. Sound, for both radio and television, is converted into electrical signals which are strengthened and then combined with a radio wave which carries them through the air.

The light from the scene to be televised is split by mirrors into the three primary colors – blue, green, and red. The light rays are converted into electrical signals by three image orthicons, and the signals are strengthened before transmission. The signals are transmitted and sorted out into the three colors by the television receiver. Electron guns in the cathode tubes fire scanning beams on to the screen, which is coated with three kinds of phosphor dots which glow blue, green, and red when struck by the beam.

Right: John Logie Baird (1888–1946), inventor of television. In 1926 he succeeded in transmitting the first moving pictures. The images flickered badly and were seen on a dim screen only a few inches high, but they marked the start of the development of television.

Exploring the Spectrum

Until the mid-19th century, men had studied only the visible part of the spectrum – light waves. But light was only one small part of a much wider band of electromagnetic waves.

Isaac Newton had shown that white light can be broken up by a prism into a spectrum of colors. By the beginning of the 19th century it was recognized that this visible spectrum was only a small part of a longer and invisible band that we call the electromagnetic spectrum. This spectrum is composed of a whole family of waves ranging from radio waves to X-rays and gamma rays.

Capturing light

The ancient Greeks were familiar with the "camera obscura" or pinhole camera, which could produce an image on a screen. Yet nobody had ever managed to capture these images in a permanent way. The first person to do so was the French inventor Louis Daguerre (1787–1851). Daguerre stumbled upon his discovery in 1839 after he had been exposing in a

camera a silvered plate coated with silver iodide in the hope of obtaining an image. The experiment failed and he put the plate away in a cupboard containing chemicals. Later he discovered that a brilliant image had appeared on the plate and that this was due to vapor that had escaped from a bottle of mercury in the cupboard.

In England William Fox Talbot (1800–1877) developed another process of photography in 1841 that became the starting point of modern photography. Talbot's "calotype" process made it possible to make as many positive prints from the original negative as might be needed. Photography became an important new tool for scientists.

The equipment of a 19th-century photographer was clumsy compared with today's cameras. He trundled his camera round on a cart, shrouding himself with the hood to take a photograph and to develop the wet-coated plates which were used until the late 19th century.

Human eyes are sensitive only to visible light. They are unable to see radio and television waves or X-rays. Yet visible light rays are only a very small segment of the entire electromagnetic spectrum.

Geiger counter

X-ray unit

sunlamp

visible spectrum

Gamma-rays	X-rays		ultra-violet	visible light		infra-
wavelength (centimeters)		10^{-8}	10^{-6}	10^{-4}		10^{-2}

Pictures of the invisible

In 1895 Wilhelm Roentgen (1845–1923), a German professor of physics, was researching the properties of cathode rays. While working with a Crookes' tube, a glass vacuum tube through which an electric current can be passed, Roentgen found that some nearby photographic plates had become fogged in spite of being inside lightproof wrappings. More astonishing were the eerie shadow pictures of the bones of Roentgen's hand that the rays cast when he held it between the tube and a fluorescent screen. Unable to explain the puzzling power of these rays or why they could only be detected by their effects on photographic plates, Roentgen named them X-rays. X being the symbol for the unknown.

A similar chance discovery was made by Antoine Henri Becquerel (1852–1908). Becquerel happened to be developing some photographic plates which he had placed in a drawer in which there were traces of a uranium compound. He was startled to see that they had been blackened by the uranium. Becquerel had discovered the existence of natural radioactivity. He also found that uranium ore was far more radioactive than uranium itself; it was this discovery that puzzled Marie Curie (1867–1934) and her husband Pierre.

Marie and Pierre Curie in their laboratory in 1903 – the year of their joint Nobel Prize.

A new radioactive element

The Curies set about isolating the other mineral in uranium ore that they believed was the source of the additional radiation. They obtained several tons of free pitchblende residues – uranium-bearing ore from which the uranium had been extracted. They began a laborious process of "cooking" the pitchblende to extract the unknown mineral and after two years produced a new radioactive element that Marie named "polonium" after her native Poland. In December 1898, they isolated a tiny quantity of a second element they called "radium". Here was a mineral that, in its pure form, proved to be a million times more radioactive than the same amount of uranium.

Antoine Henri Becquerel (1852–1908) was the discoverer of natural radiation.

The Nature of Energy and Matter

James Clerk Maxwell (1831–1879) sent his first paper, on the ''Description of Oval Curves'', to the Royal Society of Edinburgh when he was only 15.

Max Planck (1858–1947), the German physicist, proposed and developed the quantum theory of radiation.

Below: Lord Rutherford holding his original alpha-particle scattering apparatus.

Newton's laws governing the universe were modified in the 20th century by Albert Einstein – a scientist who worked not in a laboratory, but with pencil and paper.

The laws of the physical universe that were stated by Newton in the latter half of the 17th century remained unchallenged for the next two hundred years. But in the middle of the 19th century, the brilliant Scottish scientist James Clerk Maxwell said that light, and every other form of radiant energy, travels in the form of electromagnetic waves which radiate outward from their source much like the ripples that are formed by dropping a stone into a pool. Newton's disputed "corpuscular" theory of light, which maintained that light consists of tiny particles, was at least disproved – at least so it seemed.

Essential to Maxwell's wave theories was the idea of an invisible "ether" that was everywhere. Light waves were believed to be transmitted through the ether much as sound waves are transmitted by molecules in the air. But in 1887, two American scientists, Albert Michelson and Edward Morley showed that the speed of light never varies and that Clerk Maxwell's ether does not exist.

As the 19th century drew to a close, Max Planck in Berlin showed that radiation, such as light and heat, is given off in the form of tiny "packets" of energy, as well as in the form of waves. Planck called these particles quanta, but he was reluctant to believe his own theory as it disagreed with the former idea that radiation was a continuous stream of energy with a wavelike motion.

Albert Einstein established the relationship between mass and energy with his equation $E = mc^2$, where E is energy, m is mass, and c the velocity of light.

Albert Einstein and the revolution in physics

If it can be said that modern science has a man of genius, that man is undoubtedly Albert Einstein (1879–1955). Einstein has been responsible for reordering mankind's view of the universe. In 1905, he wrote a series of scientific articles that boldly swept aside the long established "facts" of Newtonian physics.

Einstein was already familiar with Planck's quantum theory when he proposed that light can also exist as bundles of energy, or photons. However, Einstein's findings did not reject Maxwell's wave theories. Rather, they showed that radiated energy was a two-faced phenomenon. Thus the nature of low-frequency radiation (radio waves) is best described in terms of waves, whereas photons are more suitable to describe high-frequency gamma and X-rays. Visible light possesses both wave and particle characteristics.

E = mc²

In 1905 Einstein outlined his famous theory of relativity. He rejected the notion that absolute measurements of movement can be made in a universe which lacks any single fixed point. All motion is therefore relative to the place at which it is measured. The only constant "fact" in the universe is the speed of light: 186,272 miles per second.

The theory of relativity also introduced the famous $E = mc^2$ equation that established the link between energy and matter. Physics had been anchored to the notion that a fixed amount of matter existed in the universe which could neither be destroyed nor added to. But Einstein's formula proved that matter and energy are two aspects of the same thing. It also showed that a tiny bit of matter could be converted into a stupendous amount of energy. One pound of matter, if totally destroyed, could yield more energy than 10 million tons of ordinary explosive. Einstein himself was cautious about his formula at first. "There is not the slightest indication that the energy will ever be obtainable. It would mean that the atom would have to be shattered at will. . . ." Yet only 40 years later, the fireball of the first atomic bomb shot into the air.

Rutherford's invisible planetary system

The difficulty in investigating atoms is that they cannot be seen even under the most powerful microscopes. In 1896 the French scientist Henri Becquerel had discovered that uranium gives off a continuous stream of rays or radiation. At once scientists began to investigate the nature of these rays. Among them was a New Zealand-born scientist, Ernest Rutherford. He established that the Curies' radium atoms were disintegrating all the time and were emitting three types of rays called alpha, beta, and gamma rays. From this discovery

Rutherford put forward a revolutionary theory concerning the nature of matter and the atom's structure.

Rutherford's model of the atom was the result of a famous experiment during which he bombarded fine sheets of gold foil with a stream of alpha particles. In 1911 he announced a new model of the atom based on his experiments. It showed that virtually all of an atom's mass is in a tiny nucleus consisting of positively charged particles known as protons. Around the nucleus, negatively charged electrons whirl in orbit like the planets around the Sun.

In the nucleus of this atom of phosphorus are 15 positively charged protons and an equal number of neutrons, which have no charge. Round the nucleus orbit 15 negatively charged electrons. It was Rutherford who first described the orbiting of the electrons around the nucleus.

Below: A characteristic mushroom cloud marks the spot of an atomic explosion.

Power from the Atom

The word atom means "the indivisible thing". But modern scientists have shown that this is very far from being an accurate description of the smallest particle of matter.

Above: Professor Niels Bohr (1885–1962), a great Danish physicist, operating a cyclotron (particle accelerator). Bohr was awarded the Nobel Prize in 1922 for his work on the structure of the hydrogen atom.

Below: An uncontrolled neclear chain reaction. Neutron "bullets" are fired at the element uranium-235, and absorbed. The uranium nucleus explodes with tremendous force, throwing out nuclei of lighter atoms like barium and krypton as well as more neutrons. These neutrons collide with other uranium nuclei, and so the process continues.

The atom is not an indivisible unit but consists of a nucleus made up of particles called protons and neutrons, surrounded by orbiting electrons. Rutherford had also shown that by bombarding the nucleus with the atomic particles emitted by radioactive substances one atom could be changed into another.

In 1934 the Italian Enrico Fermi began to bombard all the known elements with neutrons to see which would become radioactive. He found that his neutron "bullets" were more effective if he slowed them down by passing them through a "moderator" such as water. A slow neutron, said Fermi, was more

likely to react with a nucleus with which it collided, and there was more time for the reaction to take place.

In 1938 Fermi received the Nobel Prize for his work on nuclear bombardment. He went to Stockholm in Sweden

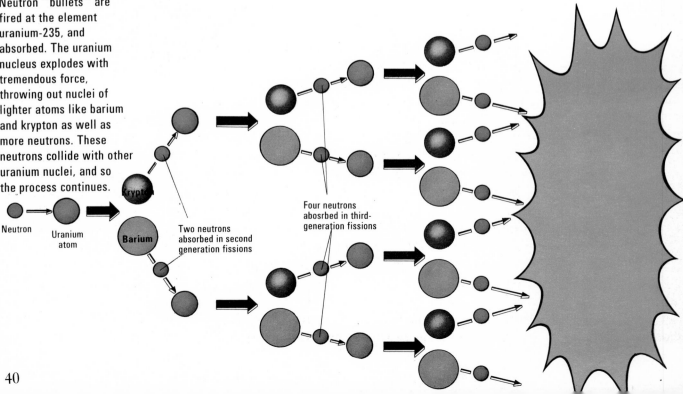

Neutron   Uranium atom   Krypton   Barium   Two neutrons absorbed in second generation fissions   Four neutrons abosrbed in third-generation fissions

Cadmium control rods

Graphite moderator

Uranium fuel rods

Steam

Heat exchanger

Concrete shield

Gas coolant

Water

Gas blower

Nuclear reactor

The nuclear reactor contains a mass of uranium which gives off neutrons, and a graphite moderator to slow down the neutrons and help the chain reaction. Cadmium rods are inserted or withdrawn to control the rate of reaction, and a liquid or gas "coolant" is driven round the reactor to draw the heat off to a heat exchanger. Here, water is heated to produce steam to drive electric generators and turbines.
Below: Enrico Fermi (1901–1954), a great Italian physicist. He produced the first nuclear chain reaction.

to receive his award – and from there sailed to the United States. For at that time Italy was under Fascist rule, and Fermi was opposed to its principles.

Controlled explosion

In 1939 the Austrian Lise Meitner showed that some of the atoms of uranium split into lighter fragments when bombarded with neutrons. The total mass of the fragments was less than that of the original atom; the missing mass must have been converted into energy, as Einstein had stated. When Fermi heard of this work he carried out experiments which indicated that the split uranium nucleus produced further neutrons. These could in turn split more uranium nuclei and, under the right conditions, the energy produced by this "chain reaction" would produce an explosion of incredible magnitude.

How could this reaction be controlled? An answer lay in the speed at which the neutrons were traveling. Most of the neutrons released in the fission (splitting) moved so fast that they failed to split other atoms. To slow them down, Fermi embedded the uranium in a mass of graphite, which acted as a moderator. Graphite tends not to absorb neutrons,

When working with radioactive materials, men wear protective clothing (above) or use remote control from behind thick screens to operate mechanical arms.

but to reflect them back into the uranium, traveling at slower speed.

It was clearly vital that the chain reaction should not proceed too fast and produce an uncontrolled reaction. Fermi overcame this problem by inserting cadmium rods in his pile of graphite. These could be moved in or out of the uranium. Cadmium absorbs slow neutrons, so by moving the cadium rods in and out Fermi could control the reaction.

In 1942 Fermi's pile was built at Chicago. It was the world's first nuclear reactor.

The New Cosmology

Above: The English astronomer James Jeans (1877–1946), one of the first advocates of a "steady state" theory of the creation of the universe.

Below: Dark patches, called sunspots, frequently appear on the Sun's surface at places where the temperature is abnormally low.
Below center: Hamason's comet, an unusually large one, seen in 1961. The tail of a comet may be over 100 million miles long. Below right: The Rosette Nebula – central stars surrounded by gas. Modern astronomy has proved that while some nebulae, like this one, are within our galaxy, others are in fact distant galaxies.

Advanced equipment revealed new mysteries in the universe.

Although the extent of the known universe during Newton's life in the 17th century was limited because of the poor quality of telescopes at the time, scientists had no great difficulty in making sense of the phenomena they observed. Newton's laws of mechanics satisfactorily explained the movements of the Sun, the Moon, and the planets. But as the horizons of the universe continued to expand, certain puzzling phenomena began to emerge.

Charting the Milky Way
A leading figure in the exploration of the frontiers of the universe was the great 18th-century astronomer, William Herschel. His painstaking improvements to the telescope provided him with a fine research tool. Among his many findings, Herschel's observations of the night sky resulted in the discovery of the planet Uranus, thus doubling the known size of the solar system, and in the charting of more than 2300 nebulae. These mysterious fuzzy patches of light were generally believed to be distant luminous dustclouds, although Herschel said that they might be huge clusters of stars similar to the Milky Way. From his

observations, Herschel recognized that the Milky Way is a distinct celestial body in its own right and that our solar system is no more than a tiny smudge of light within this vast disk of stars.

Our galaxy is a Catherine wheel of stars and star systems so vast that light takes over 40,000 years to travel across its diameter.

In the 1920s the American astronomer Edwin Hubble, working with the enormous 100-inch telescope on Mount Wilson in California, was able to discern that the light of the nebula Andromeda came from the myriad pinpoints of individual stars. Hubble's calculations showed Andromeda to be some 800,000 light years away (a considerable underestimate as it turned out), more than eight times farther than the most remote star in the Milky Way. He had shown that our galaxy is not unique.

Hubble made the startling discovery that Andromeda and all other galaxies are hurtling away from one another at speeds that become greater and greater as their distances from one another increase. He also proved that the universe is steadily expanding towards infinity in every direction, although the stars and the galaxies within it all remain the same size.

Big bang or steady state
What had caused the universe to expand in the first place? The Belgian priest, Abbé Georges Lemaître, attempted to

resolve this problem. He argued that at some distant time in the past, all the matter in the heavens was crushed together in one enormous mass. This great cosmic egg finally exploded (the big bang) spewing out matter in every direction. The galaxies of today are nothing less than the remnants of Lemaître's original "primeval atom". Unfortunately, this theory does not explain how the matter was formed or why it all accumulated in one place.

The "steady state" theory said that matter is being continuously created throughout the universe. This idea was first suggested by James Jeans in 1928 and was championed by Thomas Gold and Fred Hoyle some 25 years later. The steady state theory proposes that matter appears in the space where former galaxies, that have since moved away, were born. Thus the universe goes on recreating itself forever – out of nothing.

Recent findings in radioastronomy have tended to undermine the "steady state" idea. Quasars, which are small galaxies, present a major problem for astronomers. They are the most distant objects in space, far more luminous than ordinary galaxies, and are receding at enormous speeds at the very fringes of the observable universe. Quasars may reveal what the universe looked like very early in its evolution.

Hearing the universe

Since light is only a tiny part of a virtually limitless spectrum, it is not surprising that it is not the only form of radiation emitted by the stars. With a telescope, astronomers have been able to see distant stars, whereas with a radio telescope it is also possible to hear them. Radioastronomy has the advantage of being able to penetrate dust clouds which obscure stars. The "ear" of a radio telescope is a huge dish-like structure that can be aimed to eavesdrop on any part of the universe.

Above: The radio telescope at Jodrell Bank, England. Telescopes like this can locate stars which emit radio waves.

Below: Edward White making the first American space walk in 1965.

Below: From pictures like this of the Moon's surface and manned space flights to the Moon itself we have learned much about the Earth's only satellite, 240,000 miles away.

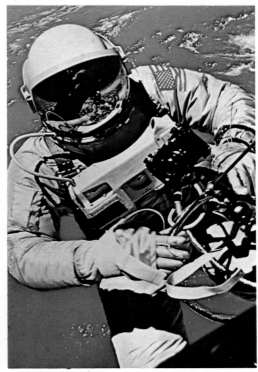

The Living Earth

The Earth under our feet feels absolutely solid and stable. But violent forces are confined beneath its surface, and even the continents themselves are slowly moving.

It is thought that the Earth, the Sun, and the other planets in the Solar System were formed about 4600 million years ago. That the world was far older than anyone had imagined was suggested by 19th century geologists – as a result of their study of rocks and fossils. The question they could not answer was how the Earth and the Solar System came into being. It is a matter still debated by scientists today.

One theory suggests that a star passed very close to the Sun and drew off a huge cloud of gas which broke into fragments

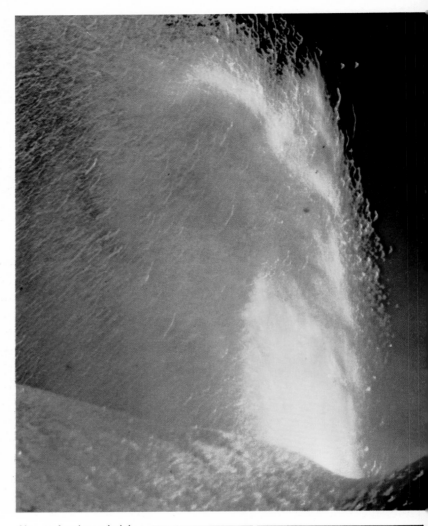

A cut-away view of the Earth, revealing its structure. It is thought that the inner core may be of solid iron. The outer core is molten iron and nickel. The semi-liquid mantle is crossed by slow currents which cause volcanoes and earth movements.

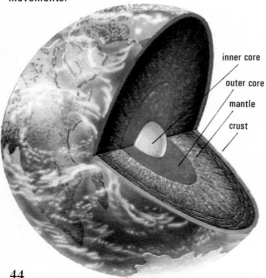

inner core

outer core

mantle

crust

Above: A volcano belches fire as a pool of magma within the Earth forces its way to the surface, erupting as red-hot lava.

Two hundred million years ago the Earth's land masses were gathered together into the huge super-continent, Pangea. About 100 million years later movements beneath the Earth's surface split up Pangea. Australia and Antarctica broke free of Africa and the Atlantic Ocean began to take shape. Today the continents continue to move, riding on huge sections of the Earth's crust called plates.

200 million years ago

100 million years ago

present day
(showing tectonic plates)

Clouds photographed from a satellite. Satellites help meteorologists to study the weather.

A fossil of an ichtyosaurus. Scientists have learned much about the Earth's history by studying the remains of prehistoric life.

and cooled into the planets of the Solar System. Another theory put forward was that the Sun once had a companion star which exploded, scattering debris which became the orbiting planets. The most probable theory was first proposed in 1796 by the French astronomer and mathematician Pierre Laplace. He maintained that there was a great cloud of dust and gas which became more and more concentrated under the influence of gravity. The center of the cloud condensed into the Sun, and other centers of concentration became the planets. Modern research seems to confirm Laplace's cloud theory.

Inside the Earth

When the Earth was formed, the force of gravity pulled the densest matter into the center to form the core. Less dense materials formed the mantle, and the least dense were forced to the outside and became the Earth's crust. Scientists have long believed that the core of the Earth is extremely hot and dense. The existence of the core was first established mathematically in the early 20th century. There is some evidence that the inner part of the core is solid, but this has never been proved.

In order to find out more about the internal structure of the Earth, scientists have bored holes into the crust and have taken rock samples. But even the deepest oil drillings only penetrate the crust, which is about 25 miles (40 km) thick under the continents. Below this crust tremendous pressures build up in the mantle – and from time to time break through the earth's surface as volcanoes and earthquakes. When a volcano erupts, molten rock, or magma, from deep inside the Earth is forced through a point of weakness to the surface. Earthquakes are caused by the sudden readjustment of the rocks in the crust, which fracture and shift. Once a line of weakness, or fault, has formed in the crust, the rocks are liable to go on shifting.

Our knowledge of the mantle and core of the Earth is gained entirely from recording and analysing the seismic (shock) waves produced by these disturbances. In 1897, John Milne produced the first seismograph – the forerunner of today's seismometers which are used to analyse earthquakes and tremors.

Shifting continents

After charts of newly explored parts of the world first appeared it was noted that the outlines of the continents, notably the east coast of South America and the west coast of Africa, looked as though they might well have once fitted together into one vast continent. Over millions of years these great land masses slowly shifted into their present positions. Recent theories have suggested that the Earth's crust is broken up into large segments, or "tectonic plates". These are in constant motion, driven by the heat and pressure inside the Earth.

Alfred Wegener, the German geophysicist who first suggested that all the continents originated from a single land mass.

Below: A meteorologist reads his instruments at Halley Bay Geophysical Observatory in Antarctica.

The Bricks of Life

How does each new generation inherit its parents' characteristics?

In 1859 Charles Darwin published his theory on the origin of animals and natural selection, but how individual animals acquired their special characteristics, and how they passed these down to their offspring, remained a mystery. He came up with the theory that all the body's cells shed tiny "gemmules" into the bloodstream, and these gemmules gathered to form the sex cells. A body cell that had been altered during life would thereafter produce similarly altered gemmules. This fitted in with the widely held belief put forward by the French naturalist Lamarck (1744–1829) that characteristics acquired during life – like huge muscles – could be passed on to offspring.

But Francis Galton proved that this

Children inherit half their genes from each parent. In this family one girl looks like her father, the other like her mother. So far, the baby most resembles his father.

This albino squirrel lacks all pigment for coloration. Its eyes appear red from tiny blood vessels, normally masked by pigmentation. Albinism is a hereditary condition, and is caused by a recessive gene; it appears only when the animal has no normal gene producing the "plans" for pigment.

was incorrect by making blood transfusions between black and white rabbits. After the transfusions, if Darwin were right, the black rabbits should have gemmules for white fur in their bloodstreams, the white rabbits gemmules for black fur. Their offspring would then be spotted. But no spotted rabbits were born. And the German August Weismann struck a death-blow to Lamarckism when he cut off the tails of several generations of mice. Every succeeding generation was born with long tails – so this "acquired characteristic" was clearly not being passed down.

Weismann's own theory was that characteristics were passed down by a special inherited substance. But he realized that it would be quite impossible for a child to inherit every characteristic from both parents. Before the substances from both parents came together in the fertilized egg, some reduction in what is passed down had to take place. Then he read some recent research on cells. Each living cell contained thread-like structures called chromosomes – exactly the same number in almost every cell of every animal of the same species. But the female's egg and the male's sperm only had *half* the normal number of chromosomes. Could the answer be that heredity was carried by chromosomes? Weismann was rightly confident that this was so, and that each offspring inherited only half of each parent's characteristics.

Chromosomes and genes

Weismann knew nothing of the work on heredity published by Gregor Mendel in 1866. But when this was rediscovered in 1900 it fitted in with his theory. Now more and more people studied the chromosomes. Some of the most important work was done by the American T. H. Morgan. He made a detailed study of the fruit-fly *Drosophila*, which has the advantages of having eight very large, easily observed chromosomes and breeding rapidly. Morgan's experiments with generations of fruit-flies and his observations of their chromosomes proved that inherited factors were indeed determined by *genes* carried by the chromosomes. Later it was discovered that sometimes these genes could be changed or "mutated" by radiation from outer space. This would give rise to what farmers had long called "sports" – creatures that for no apparent reason were different from their ancestors. All this research made it more and more clear that both Darwin and Mendel had been right.

Later research workers showed that the genes were made up of a nucleic acid, DNA, and in 1953 James Watson and Francis Crick presented a model showing the structure of DNA and explained how it could reproduce itself exactly. And this may have solved the problem of how life began, since DNA – the building bricks of life – could have been produced under the conditions which existed in the waters that covered the Earth many hundreds of millions of years ago.

The chromosomes of a human male sorted into pairs. The 23rd "pair" in the male consists of two very dissimilar chromosomes, an "x" chromosome and the "y" chromosome which determines a male.

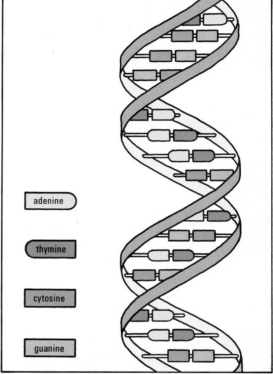

A chromosome is made of a very long double helix (spiral) of deoxyribonucleic acid or DNA. The two strands of DNA interlock with each other; each of the four units of which the strand is made up can interlock with only one other.

adenine

thymine

cytosine

guanine

The structure of the chromosome was dixcovered by James Watson and Francis Crick, who won the Nobel Prize in 1962 for their work on the structure of DNA.

Index

Acknowledgements

AEI Scientific Apparatus Ltd 25 *top right*. American Museum of Natural History 26 *center*. Heather Angel 23 *top left*, *top right*. Godfrey Argent/Royal Society 42 *top*. Atomic Energy Authority 5 *bottom right*, 39, 41 *top*, *center*, *bottom*. Dr Basil Booth/Groscience Features 44. British Antarctic Survey 45 *bottom*. British Museum 7 *top left*. Brompton Hospital 19 *bottom left*. California Institute of Technology 42 *bottom center*. California Institute of Technology/Carnegie Institute of Washington 42 *bottom right*. Camera Press 47 *bottom*. J. Allan Cash 6 *bottom*, 8 *bottom left*. Cavendish Laboratory, Cambridge 38 *top left*, *bottom*. Central Electricity Generating Board 31 *bottom*. CERN 2 *bottom*. Gene Cox Microcolour (Hunt and Broadhurst Ltd.) 33 *center*. Department of the Environment 7 *bottom*. Mary Evans Picture Library 5 *top*, 8 *top*, 15 *top bottom*, 16 *top right*, *center*, 28 *bottom*, 29 *bottom*, 32 *top*, 33 *top*, 37 *bottom right*. Michael Holford 4 *center*, 6 *top right*, 7 *top right*, 24 *top*. Michael Holford/National Gallery 4 *top*. Imitor 26 *top*, 45 *top right*, *center*. Italian Tourist Office 14 *bottom right*. Istanbul University 11 *bottom*. Jodrell Bank 43 *top*. Lockheed Solar Observatories 42 *bottom left*. Mansell Collection 5 *center*, 6 *top left*, 13 *top left*, *top right*, *bottom*, 15 *center*, 16 *bottom left*, 19 *top left*, top right, 22 *top*, 26 *bottom left*, *bottom right*, 28 *top*, 32 *center*, *bottom*, 33 *bottom*, 34 *top right*, 35 *top*, 37 *top*, 38 *top right*. Mauritshuis, The Hague 18 *top*. NASA 2 *center*, 43 *bottom left*, *bottom right*, 45 *top left*. National Portrait Gallery, London 16 *bottom right*, 19 *bottom right*. Natural Science Photos 46 *bottom*. Novosti 23 *bottom*. Peabody Museum, Yale 27 *bottom*. Pope Photography Ltd 46 *top*. Radio Times Hulton Picture Library 35 *bottom*, 38 *center*. Ronan Picture Library 8 *bottom right*, 24 *center*. Royal Danish Embassy 40. Science Museum, London 2 *bottom*, 3 *top*, 5 *center*, *bottom left*, 10 *bottom right*, 11 *top*, 14 *top left*, 16 *top left*, 18 *bottom*, 20, 24 *bottom left*, *bottom right*, 25 *top left*, *top center*, 31 *top*, 34 *top left*, 36. Michael Short/Derby Museum and Art Gallery 12, 25 *bottom*. Tate Gallery, London 3 *bottom*. Yerkes Observatory 17.

Picture Research: Penny Warn and Jackie Newton.